THE
MAP

A 10-MINUTE-A-DAY JOURNAL

C. Wair

BALBOA.
PRESS

A DIVISION OF HAY HOUSE

Balboa Press books may be ordered through booksellers or by contacting:

Balboa Press
A Division of Hay House
1663 Liberty Drive
Bloomington, IN 47403
www.balboapress.com
1 (877) 407-4847

Print information available on the last page.

ISBN: 978-1-9822-1807-2 (sc)
ISBN: 978-1-9822-1806-5 (hc)
ISBN: 978-1-9822-1854-6 (e)

Library of Congress Control Number: 2018914789

Balboa Press rev. date: 12/17/2018

For LMW
Vous êtes très aimable

CONTENTS

HOW TO USE THIS BOOK

DETERMINE YOUR PRIORITIES FOR THE YEAR

Think about the various aspects of your life that you want to work on this year. The Priorities pages list seven key facets of life as well as a blank space for you to include something specific to you. The spaces aren't too large on purpose; don't overthink or get too detailed here. Look at your goals in broad strokes.

Monthly planner

Look at the *month* ahead and see what steps you can take toward the goals you listed on the Priorities pages. Here the important thing is not to overburden yourself. "Lose 20 pounds by the end of the month" and "Find the perfect job" are not realistic goals for 30 days. A more practical entry might be

- Work on job search for an hour after work on Monday
- Start exercise Monday, 30 minutes of yoga

The point is to create an overview of the month with reasonable tasks for yourself.

Weekly Planner

While planning the month is a broad overview, the *week* will have more concrete action items.

If your monthly goal is to work on your job search and start exercising, your weekly plan might look like this

- Have a draft of resume by Wednesday; ask friends to review on Thursday
- Take a 20 min. walk during lunch at least 3 times this week

THE DAILY PAGES

IN THE MORNING

Dreams

Write down the highlights of your dreams, not necessarily in great detail, but at least the general topics and imagery. This is not meant to be a dream journal, but a chance to review the main elements. Dreams hold a great deal of uninhibited creativity that can be useful for any endeavor. Dreams also help us pinpoint the anxieties in our lives and can help hash out the issues. Use your dreams!

Steps I Will Take to Reach My Weekly Goal

Looking at your Weekly Goal page, what can you do *today* toward those goals? These should be concrete action items. Using the example above, you might write

- Walk at lunchtime
- Send resume to John to get his feedback

Try to do something, however small, toward your goal every day. Even something like looking up a topic on the web is a step forward. Writing the steps daily helps keep your intention in front of you. Don't forget that scheduling relaxation is important, too! A day "off" to rest and have fun replenishes the energy to keep working toward your goals.

At Night

Daily Summary (Or, The Brain Dump)

Jot down the major happenings of the day, including anything that bothered you, accomplishments, and general emotions. Doing this helps get you to sleep faster (no lying awake mulling things over) and it gives your dreams "room" to explore deeper issues. When you explore your dreams in the morning, you can look back at the Summary to see what may have prompted them.

The Brain Dump is anywhere from a couple of lines to a paragraph. Don't go deep; this isn't a diary. A typical entry might look something like this:

- Jane was rude to me at work; proud of how I handled it.
- Walked 2 miles
- Discovered I need new tires; worried about the expense.
- Long talk with Jo tonight. Laughed the whole time.

To-do List

Creating your to-do list before bed is to rid your mind of concerns for the next day. Try not to worry about the details. You can fine-tune the list in the morning. Again, the point is to get the big issues off of your mind before you fall asleep.

There are all sorts of guides to effective time management and apps that are helpful. No matter if you use pen and paper or an app, keep these things in mind:

- **Know your limits**. Don't over-extend yourself. It's easy to make a long list and then at the end of the day, punish yourself for not getting everything done.

- **Schedule rest, relaxation, and play.** If you pack your list with energy-consuming tasks day after day, you tend to burn out. Make sure to spend time on you—it's not a luxury; it's an investment in yourself.

Gratitude

Don't underestimate the power of gratitude. By recognizing what we already have, we improve our outlook as we pursue our goals. If you're unfamiliar with the practice, it might take a bit of time coming up with the 4 items. But once you get the hang of it, you'll soon feel the positive impact it has on your mindset.

My own first list was paltry:

> I have a roof over my head
> I didn't get fired today
> I woke up this morning
> I have books

That list may look uninspiring, but it opened a door: I was able to go sleep with a lighter heart and wake up the next day with a much brighter outlook. This was the beginning of a crucial change of mindset.

Note to self

This is a simple thought to keep in mind as you go to sleep. Something positive to take with you as you fall into dream. A mantra, prayer, or favorite quote. A simple "You can do it!" or "I'm proud of what I've accomplished!"

This is not to be something to overthink. And it's fine to repeat the note. The point is to put something in writing, making a habit of encouraging yourself. Be your own best cheerleader!

THE
JOURNAL

DETERMINE YOUR PRIORITIES

Health/Exercise

Career

Creativity

Finances

Relationships

Spiritual life

Hobbies/Leisure

_____

MONTHLY PLANNER

Week 1 Goals

Week 2 Goals

Week 3 Goals

Week 4 Goals

WEEKLY PLANNER

Weekly Goals

My Accomplishments

Special Dates/Events

MORNING

Dreams

_____

_____

_____

_____

_____

_____

_____

_____

_____

Steps I Will Take to Reach My Weekly Goal

_____

_____

_____

_____

We know what we are, but know not what we may be.
~William Shakespeare

NIGHT

Daily Summary

_____

_____

_____

_____

_____

_____

_____

_____

Tomorrow's To-Do List

_____   _____

_____   _____

_____   _____

4 Things for Which I Am Grateful

_____   _____

_____   _____

Nightly Note to Self

_____

_____

_____

_____

MORNING

Dreams

_____

_____

_____

_____

_____

_____

_____

_____

Steps I Will Take to Reach My Weekly Goal

_____

_____

_____

_____

_____

We have all a better guide in ourselves, if we would attend to it, than any other person can be.

~Jane Austen

NIGHT

Daily Summary

_____

_____

_____

_____

_____

_____

_____

_____

_____

Tomorrow's To-Do List

_____

_____

_____   _____

_____   _____

4 Things for Which You Are Grateful

_____   _____

_____   _____

Nightly Note to Self

_____

_____

_____

_____

15

MORNING

Dreams

_____

_____

_____

_____

_____

_____

_____

_____

_____

_____

Steps I Will Take to Reach My Weekly Goal

_____

_____

_____

_____

_____

What is genius but the power of expressing a new individuality?
  ~Elizabeth Barrett Browning

NIGHT

Daily Summary

_____
_____
_____
_____
_____
_____
_____
_____
_____

Tomorrow's To-Do List

_____
_____
_____   _____
_____

4 Things for Which You Are Grateful

_____   _____
_____

Nightly Note to Self

_____
_____
_____
_____

MORNING

Dreams

_____

_____

_____

_____

_____

_____

_____

_____

Steps I Will Take to Reach My Weekly Goal

_____

_____

_____

_____

_____

We have to do with the past only as we can make it useful to the present and the future.
~Frederick Douglass

NIGHT

Daily Summary

_____

_____

_____

_____

_____

_____

_____

_____

_____

Tomorrow's To-Do List

_____

_____

_____

4 Things for Which You Are Grateful

_____

_____

Nightly Note to Self

_____

_____

_____

_____

MORNING

Dreams

_____

_____

_____

_____

_____

_____

_____

_____

_____

_____

Steps I Will Take to Reach My Weekly Goal

_____

_____

_____

_____

_____

For success, attitude is equally as important as ability.
~ Walter Scott

NIGHT

Daily Summary

_____

_____

_____

_____

_____

_____

_____

_____

Tomorrow's To-Do List

_____

_____

_____   _____

_____

4 Things for Which You Are Grateful

_____   _____

_____   _____

Nightly Note to Self

_____

_____

_____

_____

MORNING

Dreams

_____

_____

_____

_____

_____

_____

_____

_____

Steps I Will Take to Reach My Weekly Goal

_____

_____

_____

_____

_____

What is right to be done cannot be done too soon.
~Jane Austen

NIGHT

Daily Summary

_____

_____

_____

_____

_____

_____

_____

_____

_____

Tomorrow's To-Do List

_____

_____

_____

_____

4 Things for Which You Are Grateful

_____

_____

Nightly Note to Self

_____

_____

_____

_____

MORNING

Dreams

_____

_____

_____

_____

_____

_____

_____

_____

_____

Steps I Will Take to Reach My Weekly Goal

_____

_____

_____

_____

_____

You, yourself, as much as anybody in the entire universe, deserve your love and affection.

~Buddha

NIGHT

Daily Summary

_____

_____

_____

_____

_____

_____

_____

_____

_____

Tomorrow's To-Do List

_____

_____

_____

_____

4 Things for Which You Are Grateful

_____

_____

Nightly Note to Self

_____

_____

_____

_____

WEEKLY PLANNER

Weekly Goals

My Accomplishments

Special Dates/Events

NOTES

MORNING

Dreams

_____
_____
_____
_____
_____
_____
_____
_____

Steps I Will Take to Reach My Weekly Goal

_____
_____
_____
_____
_____

The beginning is always today.
~Mary Wollstonecraft

NIGHT

Daily Summary

_____

_____

_____

_____

_____

_____

_____

_____

_____

Tomorrow's To-Do List

_____

_____

_____

4 Things for Which You Are Grateful

_____

_____

Nightly Note to Self

_____

_____

_____

_____

MORNING

Dreams

_____

_____

_____

_____

_____

_____

_____

_____

Steps I Will Take to Reach My Weekly Goal

_____

_____

_____

_____

It is during our darkest moments that we must focus to see the light.
~Aristotle

NIGHT

Daily Summary

_____

_____

_____

_____

_____

_____

_____

_____

_____

Tomorrow's To-Do List

_____

_____

_____   _____

_____

4 Things for Which You Are Grateful

_____   _____

_____

Nightly Note to Self

_____

_____

_____

_____

MORNING

Dreams

_____

_____

_____

_____

_____

_____

_____

_____

Steps I Will Take to Reach My Weekly Goal

_____

_____

_____

_____

Start by doing what's necessary; then do what's possible; and suddenly you are doing the impossible.

~Francis of Assisi

NIGHT

Daily Summary

_____

_____

_____

_____

_____

_____

_____

_____

_____

Tomorrow's To-Do List

_____

_____

_____

4 Things for Which You Are Grateful

_____

_____

Nightly Note to Self

_____

_____

_____

_____

MORNING

Dreams

_____

_____

_____

_____

_____

_____

_____

_____

Steps I Will Take to Reach My Weekly Goal

_____

_____

_____

_____

_____

When you arise in the morning, think of what a precious privilege it is to be alive—to breathe, to think, to enjoy, to love.
~Marcus Aurelius

NIGHT

Daily Summary

_____

_____

_____

_____

_____

_____

_____

_____

Tomorrow's To-Do List

_____

_____

_____

4 Things for Which You Are Grateful

_____

_____

Nightly Note to Self

_____

_____

_____

_____

MORNING

Dreams

_____

_____

_____

_____

_____

_____

_____

Steps I Will Take to Reach My Weekly Goal

_____

_____

_____

_____

_____

Don't judge each day by the harvest that you reap but by the seeds that you plant.

~Robert Louis Stevenson

NIGHT

Daily Summary

_____

_____

_____

_____

_____

_____

_____

_____

_____

Tomorrow's To-Do List

_____

_____

_____

_____

4 Things for Which I Am Grateful

_____

_____

Nightly Note to Self

_____

_____

_____

_____

MORNING

Dreams

_____

_____

_____

_____

_____

_____

_____

_____

Steps I Will Take to Reach My Weekly Goal

_____

_____

_____

_____

It is not in the stars to hold our destiny but in ourselves.
~William Shakespeare

NIGHT

Daily Summary

_____

_____

_____

_____

_____

_____

_____

_____

_____

Tomorrow's To-Do List

_____

_____

_____   _____

4 Things for Which I Am Grateful

_____   _____

_____   _____

Nightly Note to Self

_____

_____

_____

_____

MORNING

Dreams

_____

_____

_____

_____

_____

_____

_____

_____

_____

Steps I Will Take to Reach My Weekly Goal

_____

_____

_____

_____

_____

For success, attitude is equally as important as ability.
~ Walter Scott

NIGHT

Daily Summary

_____
_____
_____
_____
_____
_____
_____
_____
_____

Tomorrow's To-Do List

_____
_____
_____ _____

4 Things for Which I Am Grateful

_____ _____
_____

Nightly Note to Self

_____
_____
_____
_____

WEEKLY PLANNER

Weekly Goals

My Accomplishments

Special Dates/Events

NOTES

MORNING

Dreams

_____

_____

_____

_____

_____

_____

_____

_____

_____

Steps I Will Take to Reach My Weekly Goal

_____

_____

_____

_____

If opportunity doesn't knock, build a door.
~Milton Berle

NIGHT

Daily Summary

_____
_____
_____
_____
_____
_____
_____
_____
_____

Tomorrow's To-Do List

_____
_____
_____ _____
_____

4 Things for Which I Am Grateful

_____ _____
_____

Nightly Note to Self

_____
_____
_____
_____

MORNING

Dreams

_____

_____

_____

_____

_____

_____

_____

Steps I Will Take to Reach My Weekly Goal

_____

_____

_____

_____

Change your thoughts and you change your world.
~Norman Vincent Peale

NIGHT

Daily Summary

_____

_____

_____

_____

_____

_____

_____

_____

_____

Tomorrow's To-Do List

_____   _____

_____   _____

_____   _____

4 Things for Which I Am Grateful

_____   _____

_____   _____

Nightly Note to Self

_____

_____

_____

_____

MORNING

Dreams

_____
_____
_____
_____
_____
_____
_____
_____
_____

Steps I Will Take to Reach My Weekly Goal

_____
_____
_____
_____
_____

Experience is the teacher of all things.
~ Julius Caesar

NIGHT

Daily Summary

_____
_____
_____
_____
_____
_____

Tomorrow's To-Do List

_____
_____
_____

4 Things for Which I Am Grateful

_____
_____

Nightly Note to Self

_____
_____
_____
_____

MORNING

Dreams

_____

_____

_____

_____

_____

_____

_____

_____

Steps I Will Take to Reach My Weekly Goal

_____

_____

_____

_____

Who seeks shall find.
    ~Sophocles

NIGHT

Daily Summary

_____

_____

_____

_____

_____

_____

_____

_____

_____

Tomorrow's To-Do List

_____

_____

_____

4 Things for Which I Am Grateful

_____

_____

Nightly Note to Self

_____

_____

_____

_____

MORNING

Dreams

_____

_____

_____

_____

_____

_____

_____

_____

Steps I Will Take to Reach My Weekly Goal

_____

_____

_____

_____

Health is the greatest gift, contentment the greatest wealth, faithfulness the best relationship.
~Buddha

NIGHT

Daily Summary

_____

_____

_____

_____

_____

_____

_____

_____

_____

Tomorrow's To-Do List

_____

_____

_____

_____

4 Things for Which I Am Grateful

_____

_____

Nightly Note to Self

_____

_____

_____

_____

MORNING

Dreams

_____

_____

_____

_____

_____

_____

_____

_____

Steps I Will Take to Reach My Weekly Goal

_____

_____

_____

_____

You were made perfectly to be loved
  ~Elizabeth Barrett Browning

NIGHT

Daily Summary

_____

_____

_____

_____

_____

_____

_____

_____

_____

Tomorrow's To-Do List

_____

_____

_____

_____

4 Things for Which I Am Grateful

_____

_____

Nightly Note to Self

_____

_____

_____

_____

MORNING

Dreams

_____

_____

_____

_____

_____

_____

_____

_____

_____

Steps I Will Take to Reach My Weekly Goal

_____

_____

_____

_____

Grace is not part of consciousness; it is the amount of light in our souls, not knowledge nor reason.

~Pope Francis

NIGHT

Daily Summary

_____
_____
_____
_____
_____
_____
_____
_____
_____
_____

Tomorrow's To-Do List

_____
_____
_____
_____

4 Things for Which I Am Grateful

_____
_____

Nightly Note to Self

_____
_____
_____
_____

WEEKLY PLANNER

Weekly Goals

My Accomplishments

Special Dates/Events

NOTES

MORNING

Dreams

_____

_____

_____

_____

_____

_____

_____

_____

Steps I Will Take to Reach My Weekly Goal

_____

_____

_____

_____

That best portion of a good man's life,—
His little, nameless, unremembered acts
Of kindness and of love.

~William Wordsworth

NIGHT

Daily Summary

_____

_____

_____

_____

_____

_____

_____

_____

Tomorrow's To-Do List

_____

_____

_____

4 Things for Which I Am Grateful

_____

_____

Nightly Note to Self

_____

_____

_____

_____

MORNING

Dreams

_____

_____

_____

_____

_____

_____

_____

Steps I Will Take to Reach My Weekly Goal

_____

_____

_____

_____

Keep your face always toward the sunshine—and shadows will fall behind you.
    ~Walt Whitman

NIGHT

Daily Summary

_____

_____

_____

_____

_____

_____

_____

_____

Tomorrow's To-Do List

_____

_____

_____   _____

_____

4 Things for Which I Am Grateful

_____   _____

_____

Nightly Note to Self

_____

_____

_____

_____

MORNING

Dreams

_____

_____

_____

_____

_____

_____

_____

_____

_____

Steps I Will Take to Reach My Weekly Goal

_____

_____

_____

_____

_____

Believe you can and you're halfway there.
~Theodore Roosevelt

NIGHT

Daily Summary

_____

_____

_____

_____

_____

_____

_____

_____

Tomorrow's To-Do List

_____

_____

_____

_____

4 Things for Which I Am Grateful

_____

_____

Nightly Note to Self

_____

_____

_____

_____

MORNING

Dreams

_____

_____

_____

_____

_____

_____

_____

_____

_____

Steps I Will Take to Reach My Weekly Goal

_____

_____

_____

_____

No act of kindness, no matter how small, is ever wasted.
~Aesop

NIGHT

Daily Summary

_____

_____

_____

_____

_____

_____

_____

_____

Tomorrow's To-Do List

_____

_____

_____ _____

_____

4 Things for Which I Am Grateful

_____ _____

_____

Nightly Note to Self

_____

_____

_____

_____

MORNING

Dreams

_____

_____

_____

_____

_____

_____

_____

_____

_____

Steps I Will Take to Reach My Weekly Goal

_____

_____

_____

_____

_____

If the world seems cold to you, kindle fires to warm it.
~Lucy Larcom

NIGHT

Daily Summary

_____

_____

_____

_____

_____

_____

_____

_____

Tomorrow's To-Do List

_____

_____

_____

4 Things for Which I Am Grateful

_____

_____

Nightly Note to Self

_____

_____

_____

_____

MORNING

Dreams

_____

_____

_____

_____

_____

_____

_____

_____

Steps I Will Take to Reach My Weekly Goal

_____

_____

_____

_____

_____

Well-ordered self-love is right and natural.
~Thomas Aquinas

NIGHT

Daily Summary

_____

_____

_____

_____

_____

_____

_____

_____

_____

Tomorrow's To-Do List

_____

_____

_____   _____

_____

4 Things for Which I Am Grateful

_____   _____

_____

Nightly Note to Self

_____

_____

_____

_____

MORNING

Dreams

_____

_____

_____

_____

_____

_____

_____

_____

_____

Steps I Will Take to Reach My Weekly Goal

_____

_____

_____

_____

What we think, we become.
   ~Buddha

NIGHT

Daily Summary

_____
_____
_____
_____
_____
_____
_____
_____
_____

Tomorrow's To-Do List

_____   _____
_____   _____
_____   _____
_____

4 Things for Which I Am Grateful

_____   _____
_____

Nightly Note to Self

_____
_____
_____
_____

MONTHLY PLANNER

Week 1 Goals

Week 2 Goals

Week 3 Goals

Week 4 Goals

WEEKLY PLANNER

Weekly Goals

My Accomplishments

Special Dates/Events

MORNING

Dreams

_____

_____

_____

_____

_____

_____

_____

_____

Steps I Will Take to Reach My Weekly Goal

_____

_____

_____

_____

_____

Don't judge each day by the harvest you reap but by the seeds that you plant.

~Robert Louis Stevenson

NIGHT

Daily Summary

_____

_____

_____

_____

_____

_____

_____

Tomorrow's To-Do List

_____

_____

_____ _____

_____

4 Things for Which I Am Grateful

_____ _____

_____

Nightly Note to Self

_____

_____

_____

_____

MORNING

Dreams

_____

_____

_____

_____

_____

_____

_____

_____

Steps I Will Take to Reach My Weekly Goal

_____

_____

_____

_____

_____

If you're not getting the things you want, need, or desire, it's because you have not accepted that you can have them.
~Della Reese

NIGHT

Daily Summary

_____

_____

_____

_____

_____

_____

_____

_____

Tomorrow's To-Do List

_____

_____

_____

4 Things for Which I Am Grateful

_____

_____

Nightly Note to Self

_____

_____

_____

_____

MORNING

Dreams

_____

_____

_____

_____

_____

_____

_____

_____

Steps I Will Take to Reach My Weekly Goal

_____

_____

_____

_____

_____

There are no strangers here; Only friends you haven't yet met.
~William Butler Yeats

NIGHT

Daily Summary

_____

_____

_____

_____

_____

_____

_____

_____

Tomorrow's To-Do List

_____

_____

_____

_____

4 Things for Which I Am Grateful

_____

_____

Nightly Note to Self

_____

_____

_____

_____

MORNING

Dreams

_____

_____

_____

_____

_____

_____

_____

_____

_____

Steps I Will Take to Reach My Weekly Goal

_____

_____

_____

_____

Humanity, take a good look at yourself. Inside, you've got heaven and earth, and all of creation. You're a world—everything is hidden in you.

~Hildegard of Bingen

NIGHT

Daily Summary

_____
_____
_____
_____
_____
_____
_____
_____
_____

Tomorrow's To-Do List

_____
_____
_____

4 Things for Which I Am Grateful

_____
_____

Nightly Note to Self

_____
_____
_____
_____

MORNING

Dreams

_____

_____

_____

_____

_____

_____

_____

_____

_____

Steps I Will Take to Reach My Weekly Goal

_____

_____

_____

_____

_____

All you need is the plan, the road map, and the courage to press on to your destination.
~Earl Nightingale

NIGHT

Daily Summary

_____

_____

_____

_____

_____

_____

_____

_____

_____

Tomorrow's To-Do List

_____

_____

_____

_____

4 Things for Which I Am Grateful

_____

_____

Nightly Note to Self

_____

_____

_____

_____

MORNING

Dreams

_____

_____

_____

_____

_____

_____

_____

_____

_____

Steps I Will Take to Reach My Weekly Goal

_____

_____

_____

_____

It takes as much energy to wish as it does to plan.
~Eleanor Roosevelt

NIGHT

Daily Summary

_____

_____

_____

_____

_____

_____

_____

_____

Tomorrow's To-Do List

_____

_____

_____

4 Things for Which I Am Grateful

_____

_____

Nightly Note to Self

_____

_____

_____

_____

MORNING

Dreams

_____

_____

_____

_____

_____

_____

_____

Steps I Will Take to Reach My Weekly Goal

_____

_____

_____

_____

There is nothing on this earth more to be prized than true friendship.

~Thomas Aquinas

NIGHT

Daily Summary

_____
_____
_____
_____
_____
_____
_____
_____
_____

Tomorrow's To-Do List

_____
_____
_____

4 Things for Which I Am Grateful

_____
_____

Nightly Note to Self

_____
_____
_____
_____

WEEKLY PLANNER

Weekly Goals

My Accomplishments

Special Dates/Events

NOTES

MORNING

Dreams

_____

_____

_____

_____

_____

_____

_____

_____

Steps I Will Take to Reach My Weekly Goal

_____

_____

_____

_____

_____

As we express our gratitude, we must never forget that the highest appreciation is not to utter words, but to live by them.
~John F. Kennedy

NIGHT

Daily Summary

_____

_____

_____

_____

_____

_____

_____

_____

Tomorrow's To-Do List

_____   _____

_____   _____

4 Things for Which I Am Grateful

_____   _____

_____

Nightly Note to Self

_____

_____

_____

_____

MORNING

Dreams

_____

_____

_____

_____

_____

_____

_____

_____

Steps I Will Take to Reach My Weekly Goal

_____

_____

_____

_____

Do not wait to strike till the iron is hot; but make it hot by striking.
  ~William Butler Yeats

NIGHT

Daily Summary

_____

_____

_____

_____

_____

_____

_____

_____

_____

Tomorrow's To-Do List

_____

_____

_____

_____

4 Things for Which I Am Grateful

_____

_____

Nightly Note to Self

_____

_____

_____

_____

MORNING

Dreams

_____

_____

_____

_____

_____

_____

_____

Steps I Will Take to Reach My Weekly Goal

_____

_____

_____

_____

If you believe in yourself and have dedication and pride—and never quit, you'll be a winner. The price of victory is high but so are the rewards.

~Paul Bryant

NIGHT

Daily Summary

_____
_____
_____
_____
_____
_____
_____
_____

Tomorrow's To-Do List

_____
_____
_____

4 Things for Which I Am Grateful

_____
_____

Nightly Note to Self

_____
_____
_____
_____

MORNING

Dreams

_____
_____
_____
_____
_____
_____
_____

Steps I Will Take to Reach My Weekly Goal

_____
_____
_____
_____

If your actions inspire others to dream more, learn more, do
more and become more, you are a leader.

~ John Quincy Adams

NIGHT

Daily Summary

_____

_____

_____

_____

_____

_____

_____

_____

Tomorrow's To-Do List

_____

_____

_____   _____

_____

4 Things for Which I Am Grateful

_____   _____

_____   _____

Nightly Note to Self

_____

_____

_____

_____

MORNING

Dreams

_____

_____

_____

_____

_____

_____

_____

_____

Steps I Will Take to Reach My Weekly Goal

_____

_____

_____

_____

_____

You must do the things you think you cannot do.
~Eleanor Roosevelt

NIGHT

Daily Summary

_____

_____

_____

_____

_____

_____

_____

_____

Tomorrow's To-Do List

_____

_____

_____

4 Things for Which I Am Grateful

_____

_____

Nightly Note to Self

_____

_____

_____

_____

MORNING

Dreams

_____

_____

_____

_____

_____

_____

_____

_____

Steps I Will Take to Reach My Weekly Goal

_____

_____

_____

_____

_____

Turn your face to the sun and the shadows fall behind you.
   ~Unknown

NIGHT

Daily Summary

_____
_____
_____
_____
_____
_____
_____

Tomorrow's To-Do List

_____
_____
_____
_____

4 Things for Which I Am Grateful

_____
_____

Nightly Note to Self

_____
_____
_____
_____

MORNING

Dreams

Steps I Will Take to Reach My Weekly Goal

That best portion of a good man's life,—
His little, nameless, unremembered acts
Of kindness and of love.
　　~William Wordsworth

NIGHT

Daily Summary

_____

_____

_____

_____

_____

_____

_____

_____

_____

Tomorrow's To-Do List

_____

_____

_____

4 Things for Which I Am Grateful

_____

_____

Nightly Note to Self

_____

_____

_____

_____

WEEKLY PLANNER

Weekly Goals

My Accomplishments

Special Dates/Events

NOTES

MORNING

Dreams

_____

_____

_____

_____

_____

_____

_____

Steps I Will Take to Reach My Weekly Goal

_____

_____

_____

_____

With mirth and laughter let old wrinkles come.
~William Shakespeare

NIGHT

Daily Summary

_____

_____

_____

_____

_____

_____

_____

_____

Tomorrow's To-Do List

_____

_____

_____

_____

4 Things for Which I Am Grateful

_____

_____

Nightly Note to Self

_____

_____

_____

_____

MORNING

Dreams

_____

_____

_____

_____

_____

_____

_____

_____

_____

Steps I Will Take to Reach My Weekly Goal

_____

_____

_____

_____

Happiness is neither virtue nor pleasure nor this thing nor that
but simply growth, We are happy when we are growing.
~William Butler Yeats

NIGHT

Daily Summary

_____

_____

_____

_____

_____

_____

_____

_____

Tomorrow's To-Do List

_____

_____

_____

4 Things for Which I Am Grateful

_____

_____

Nightly Note to Self

_____

_____

_____

MORNING

Dreams

_____
_____
_____
_____
_____
_____
_____
_____

Steps I Will Take to Reach My Weekly Goal

_____
_____
_____
_____
_____

With the new day comes new strength and new thoughts.
    ~Eleanor Roosevelt

NIGHT

Daily Summary

Tomorrow's To-Do List

---

4 Things for Which I Am Grateful

Nightly Note to Self

MORNING

Dreams

_____

_____

_____

_____

_____

_____

_____

_____

Steps I Will Take to Reach My Weekly Goal

_____

_____

_____

_____

_____

There is nothing impossible to him who will try.
~Alexander the Great

NIGHT

Daily Summary

_____

_____

_____

_____

_____

_____

_____

Tomorrow's To-Do List

_____

_____

_____

4 Things for Which I Am Grateful

_____

_____

Nightly Note to Self

_____

_____

_____

_____

MORNING

Dreams

_____

_____

_____

_____

_____

_____

_____

_____

Steps I Will Take to Reach My Weekly Goal

_____

_____

_____

_____

_____

Hope is being able to see that there is light despite all of the darkness.

~Desmond Tutu

NIGHT

Daily Summary

_____
_____
_____
_____
_____
_____
_____
_____

Tomorrow's To-Do List

_____
_____
_____

4 Things for Which I Am Grateful

_____
_____

Nightly Note to Self

_____
_____
_____
_____

MORNING

Dreams

_____
_____
_____
_____
_____
_____
_____
_____

Steps I Will Take to Reach My Weekly Goal

_____
_____
_____
_____

Two roads diverged in a wood and I - I took the one less traveled by, and that has made all the difference.

~Robert Frost

NIGHT

Daily Summary

_____

_____

_____

_____

_____

_____

_____

_____

Tomorrow's To-Do List

_____

_____

_____

4 Things for Which I Am Grateful

_____

_____

Nightly Note to Self

_____

_____

_____

_____

MORNING

Dreams

_____
_____
_____
_____
_____
_____
_____
_____

Steps I Will Take to Reach My Weekly Goal

_____
_____
_____
_____
_____

Ninety-nine percent of the failures come from people who have the habit of making excuses.

~George Washington Carver

NIGHT

Daily Summary

_____

_____

_____

_____

_____

_____

_____

_____

Tomorrow's To-Do List

_____

_____

_____

_____

4 Things for Which I Am Grateful

_____

_____

Nightly Note to Self

_____

_____

_____

_____

WEEKLY PLANNER

Weekly Goals

My Accomplishments

Special Dates/Events

NOTES

MORNING

Dreams

_____

_____

_____

_____

_____

_____

_____

_____

Steps I Will Take to Reach My Weekly Goal

_____

_____

_____

_____

The power of imagination makes us infinite.
~John Muir

NIGHT

Daily Summary

_____

_____

_____

_____

_____

_____

_____

_____

_____

Tomorrow's To-Do List

_____

_____

_____   _____

4 Things for Which I Am Grateful

_____   _____

_____

Nightly Note to Self

_____

_____

_____

_____

MORNING

Dreams

_____

_____

_____

_____

_____

_____

_____

Steps I Will Take to Reach My Weekly Goal

_____

_____

_____

_____

Give light, and the darkness will disappear of itself.
  ~Desiderius Erasmus

NIGHT

Daily Summary

_____

_____

_____

_____

_____

_____

_____

_____

_____

Tomorrow's To-Do List

_____   _____

_____   _____

_____   _____

4 Things for Which I Am Grateful

_____   _____

_____   _____

Nightly Note to Self

_____

_____

_____

_____

MORNING

Dreams

_____

_____

_____

_____

_____

_____

_____

_____

Steps I Will Take to Reach My Weekly Goal

_____

_____

_____

_____

Self-love is always the mainspring, more or less concealed, of our actions; it is the wind which swells the sails, without which the ship could not go.

~Emilie du Chatelet

NIGHT

Daily Summary

_____

_____

_____

_____

_____

_____

_____

_____

_____

Tomorrow's To-Do List

_____ _____

_____ _____

_____ _____

4 Things for Which I Am Grateful

_____ _____

_____ _____

Nightly Note to Self

_____

_____

_____

_____

MORNING

Dreams

_____

_____

_____

_____

_____

_____

_____

_____

_____

_____

Steps I Will Take to Reach My Weekly Goal

_____

_____

_____

_____

There is nothing either good or bad but thinking makes it so.
~William Shakespeare

NIGHT

Daily Summary

_____

_____

_____

_____

_____

_____

_____

_____

Tomorrow's To-Do List

_____

_____

_____

_____

4 Things for Which I Am Grateful

_____

_____

Nightly Note to Self

_____

_____

_____

_____

MORNING

Dreams

_____

_____

_____

_____

_____

_____

_____

_____

Steps I Will Take to Reach My Weekly Goal

_____

_____

_____

_____

_____

If we did all the things we are capable of, we would literally
astound ourselves.

~Thomas A. Edison

NIGHT

Daily Summary

_____

_____

_____

_____

_____

_____

_____

_____

Tomorrow's To-Do List

_____

_____

_____

_____

4 Things for Which I Am Grateful

_____

_____

Nightly Note to Self

_____

_____

_____

_____

MORNING

Dreams

_____

_____

_____

_____

_____

_____

_____

_____

Steps I Will Take to Reach My Weekly Goal

_____

_____

_____

_____

If I can stop one heart from breaking, I shall not live in vain.
~Emily Dickinson

NIGHT

Daily Summary

_____

_____

_____

_____

_____

_____

_____

_____

_____

Tomorrow's To-Do List

_____

_____

_____

4 Things for Which I Am Grateful

_____

_____

Nightly Note to Self

_____

_____

_____

_____

MORNING

Dreams

_____

_____

_____

_____

_____

_____

_____

_____

Steps I Will Take to Reach My Weekly Goal

_____

_____

_____

_____

_____

Habits change into character.
~Ovid

NIGHT

Daily Summary

_____

_____

_____

_____

_____

_____

_____

_____

Tomorrow's To-Do List

_____

_____

_____

_____

4 Things for Which I Am Grateful

_____

_____

Nightly Note to Self

_____

_____

_____

_____

MONTHLY PLANNER

Week 1 Goals

Week 2 Goals

Week 3 Goals

Week 4 Goals

WEEKLY PLANNER

Weekly Goals

My Accomplishments

Special Dates/Events

MORNING

Dreams

_____

_____

_____

_____

_____

_____

_____

_____

Steps I Will Take to Reach My Weekly Goal

_____

_____

_____

_____

The things that we love tell us what we are.
    ~Thomas Aquinas

NIGHT

Daily Summary

_____

_____

_____

_____

_____

_____

_____

_____

Tomorrow's To-Do List

_____

_____

_____   _____

4 Things for Which I Am Grateful

_____   _____

Nightly Note to Self

_____

_____

_____

_____

MORNING

Dreams

_____

_____

_____

_____

_____

_____

_____

_____

_____

Steps I Will Take to Reach My Weekly Goal

_____

_____

_____

_____

_____

No man's error becomes his own Law; nor obliges him to persist in it.

~Thomas Hobbes

NIGHT

Daily Summary

_____

_____

_____

_____

_____

_____

_____

Tomorrow's To-Do List

_____

_____

_____

4 Things for Which I Am Grateful

_____

_____

Nightly Note to Self

_____

_____

_____

_____

MORNING

Dreams

_____

_____

_____

_____

_____

_____

_____

_____

Steps I Will Take to Reach My Weekly Goal

_____

_____

_____

_____

The world is full of magical things patiently waiting for our wits to grow sharper.

~Bertrand Russell

NIGHT

Daily Summary

_____
_____
_____
_____
_____
_____
_____
_____

Tomorrow's To-Do List

_____   _____
_____   _____
_____   _____

4 Things for Which I Am Grateful

_____   _____
_____   _____

Nightly Note to Self

_____
_____
_____
_____

MORNING

Dreams

Steps I Will Take to Reach My Weekly Goal

Live your beliefs and you can turn the world around.
~Henry David Thoreau

NIGHT

Daily Summary

_____

_____

_____

_____

_____

_____

_____

_____

Tomorrow's To-Do List

_____

_____

_____

_____

4 Things for Which I Am Grateful

_____

_____

Nightly Note to Self

_____

_____

_____

_____

MORNING

Dreams

_____

_____

_____

_____

_____

_____

Steps I Will Take to Reach My Weekly Goal

_____

_____

_____

_____

The future belongs to those who believe in the beauty of their dreams.

~Eleanor Roosevelt

NIGHT

Daily Summary

_____

_____

_____

_____

_____

_____

_____

Tomorrow's To-Do List

_____

_____

_____

_____

4 Things for Which I Am Grateful

_____

_____

Nightly Note to Self

_____

_____

_____

_____

MORNING

Dreams

_____

_____

_____

_____

_____

_____

Steps I Will Take to Reach My Weekly Goal

_____

_____

_____

_____

From a small seed a mighty trunk may grow.
~Aeschylus

NIGHT

Daily Summary

_____

_____

_____

_____

_____

_____

_____

_____

_____

Tomorrow's To-Do List

_____

_____

_____

4 Things for Which I Am Grateful

_____

_____

Nightly Note to Self

_____

_____

_____

_____

MORNING

Dreams

_____

_____

_____

_____

_____

_____

_____

_____

Steps I Will Take to Reach My Weekly Goal

_____

_____

_____

_____

Great works are performed not by strength but by perseverance.
~Samuel Johnson

NIGHT

Daily Summary

_____

_____

_____

_____

_____

_____

_____

_____

Tomorrow's To-Do List

_____

_____

_____

_____

4 Things for Which I Am Grateful

_____

_____

Nightly Note to Self

_____

_____

_____

_____

WEEKLY PLANNER

Weekly Goals

My Accomplishments

Special Dates/Events

NOTES

MORNING

Dreams

_____
_____
_____
_____
_____
_____
_____
_____
_____

Steps I Will Take to Reach My Weekly Goal

_____
_____
_____
_____

Cherish your visions and your dreams as they are the children of your soul, the blueprints of your ultimate achievements.
    ~Napoleon Hill

NIGHT

Daily Summary

_____

_____

_____

_____

_____

_____

_____

_____

Tomorrow's To-Do List

_____

_____

_____

4 Things for Which I Am Grateful

_____

_____

Nightly Note to Self

_____

_____

_____

_____

MORNING

Dreams

_____

_____

_____

_____

_____

_____

_____

_____

Steps I Will Take to Reach My Weekly Goal

_____

_____

_____

_____

_____

What great thing would you attempt if you knew you could not fail?
~Robert H. Schuller

NIGHT

Daily Summary

_____
_____
_____
_____
_____
_____
_____
_____

Tomorrow's To-Do List

_____
_____
_____
_____

4 Things for Which I Am Grateful

_____
_____

Nightly Note to Self

_____
_____
_____
_____

MORNING

Dreams

_____

_____

_____

_____

_____

_____

_____

_____

Steps I Will Take to Reach My Weekly Goal

_____

_____

_____

_____

I dwell in possibility.
~Emily Dickinson

NIGHT

Daily Summary

_____

_____

_____

_____

_____

_____

_____

_____

Tomorrow's To-Do List

_____

_____

_____

_____

4 Things for Which I Am Grateful

_____

_____

Nightly Note to Self

_____

_____

_____

_____

MORNING

Dreams

_____

_____

_____

_____

_____

_____

_____

_____

_____

Steps I Will Take to Reach My Weekly Goal

_____

_____

_____

_____

_____

Our doubts are traitors and make us lose the good we oft might win by fearing to attempt.

~William Shakespeare

NIGHT

Daily Summary

_____

_____

_____

_____

_____

_____

_____

Tomorrow's To-Do List

_____

_____

_____

4 Things for Which I Am Grateful

_____

_____

Nightly Note to Self

_____

_____

_____

_____

MORNING

Dreams

_____

_____

_____

_____

_____

_____

_____

_____

Steps I Will Take to Reach My Weekly Goal

_____

_____

_____

_____

From what we get, we can make a living; what we give, however,
makes a life.
   ~Arthur Ashe

NIGHT

Daily Summary

_____

_____

_____

_____

_____

_____

_____

_____

Tomorrow's To-Do List

_____

_____

_____

_____

4 Things for Which I Am Grateful

_____

_____

Nightly Note to Self

_____

_____

_____

_____

MORNING

Dreams

_____

_____

_____

_____

_____

_____

_____

_____

Steps I Will Take to Reach My Weekly Goal

_____

_____

_____

_____

_____

Vitality shows in not only the ability to persist but the ability to start over.

~F. Scott Fitzgerald

NIGHT

Daily Summary

_____
_____
_____
_____
_____
_____
_____
_____
_____

Tomorrow's To-Do List

_____
_____
_____
_____

4 Things for Which I Am Grateful

_____
_____

Nightly Note to Self

_____
_____
_____
_____

MORNING

Dreams

_____

_____

_____

_____

_____

_____

_____

_____

Steps I Will Take to Reach My Weekly Goal

_____

_____

_____

_____

_____

Nurture your minds with great thoughts. To believe in the heroic makes heroes.

~Benjamin Disraeli

NIGHT

Daily Summary

_____

_____

_____

_____

_____

_____

_____

_____

Tomorrow's To-Do List

_____

_____

_____

4 Things for Which I Am Grateful

_____

_____

Nightly Note to Self

_____

_____

_____

_____

WEEKLY PLANNER

Weekly Goals

My Accomplishments

Special Dates/Events

NOTES

MORNING

Dreams

_____

_____

_____

_____

_____

_____

_____

_____

Steps I Will Take to Reach My Weekly Goal

_____

_____

_____

_____

What we achieve inwardly will change outer reality.
~Plutarch

NIGHT

Daily Summary

_____
_____
_____
_____
_____
_____
_____
_____

Tomorrow's To-Do List

_____
_____
_____
_____

4 Things for Which I Am Grateful

_____
_____

Nightly Note to Self

_____
_____
_____
_____

MORNING

Dreams

_____

_____

_____

_____

_____

_____

_____

_____

Steps I Will Take to Reach My Weekly Goal

_____

_____

_____

_____

_____

Give light and people will find the way.
~Ella Baker

NIGHT

Daily Summary

_____

_____

_____

_____

_____

_____

_____

_____

_____

Tomorrow's To-Do List

_____

_____

_____

_____

4 Things for Which I Am Grateful

_____

_____

Nightly Note to Self

_____

_____

_____

_____

MORNING

Dreams

_____

_____

_____

_____

_____

_____

_____

_____

Steps I Will Take to Reach My Weekly Goal

_____

_____

_____

_____

Ah, but a man's reach should exceed his grasp, Or what's a heaven for?

~Robert Browning

NIGHT

Daily Summary

_____
_____
_____
_____
_____
_____
_____
_____

Tomorrow's To-Do List

_____
_____
_____ _____
_____

4 Things for Which I Am Grateful

_____ _____

Nightly Note to Self

_____
_____
_____
_____

MORNING

Dreams

_____

_____

_____

_____

_____

_____

_____

_____

Steps I Will Take to Reach My Weekly Goal

_____

_____

_____

_____

Patience and perseverance have a magical effect before which difficulties disappear and obstacles vanish.

~John Quincy Adams

NIGHT

Daily Summary

_____

_____

_____

_____

_____

_____

_____

_____

_____

Tomorrow's To-Do List

_____

_____

_____   _____

4 Things for Which I Am Grateful

_____   _____

_____   _____

Nightly Note to Self

_____

_____

_____

_____

MORNING

Dreams

_____

_____

_____

_____

_____

_____

_____

_____

Steps I Will Take to Reach My Weekly Goal

_____

_____

_____

_____

Light tomorrow with today!
~Elizabeth Barrett Browning

NIGHT

Daily Summary

_____
_____
_____
_____
_____
_____
_____
_____

Tomorrow's To-Do List

_____
_____
_____
_____

4 Things for Which I Am Grateful

_____
_____

Nightly Note to Self

_____
_____
_____
_____

MORNING

Dreams

_____

_____

_____

_____

_____

_____

_____

_____

Steps I Will Take to Reach My Weekly Goal

_____

_____

_____

_____

We have it in our power to begin the world over again.
~Thomas Paine

NIGHT

Daily Summary

_____

_____

_____

_____

_____

_____

_____

Tomorrow's To-Do List

_____

_____

_____

4 Things for Which I Am Grateful

_____

_____

Nightly Note to Self

_____

_____

_____

_____

MORNING

Dreams

_____

_____

_____

_____

_____

_____

_____

_____

Steps I Will Take to Reach My Weekly Goal

_____

_____

_____

_____

We must have perseverance and above all confidence in ourselves. We must believe that we are gifted for something and that this thing must be attained.

~Marie Curie

NIGHT

Daily Summary

_____

_____

_____

_____

_____

_____

_____

_____

Tomorrow's To-Do List

_____

_____

_____

4 Things for Which I Am Grateful

_____

_____

Nightly Note to Self

_____

_____

_____

_____

WEEKLY PLANNER

Weekly Goals

My Accomplishments

Special Dates/Events

NOTES

MORNING

Dreams

_____

_____

_____

_____

_____

_____

_____

Steps I Will Take to Reach My Weekly Goal

_____

_____

_____

_____

To begin, begin.
~William Wordsworth

NIGHT

Daily Summary

_____

_____

_____

_____

_____

_____

_____

_____

_____

Tomorrow's To-Do List

_____

_____

_____

4 Things for Which I Am Grateful

_____

_____

Nightly Note to Self

_____

_____

_____

_____

MORNING

Dreams

_____

_____

_____

_____

_____

_____

_____

_____

Steps I Will Take to Reach My Weekly Goal

_____

_____

_____

_____

It is always the simple that produces the marvelous.
    ~Amelia Barr

NIGHT

Daily Summary

_____

_____

_____

_____

_____

_____

Tomorrow's To-Do List

_____

_____

_____

4 Things for Which I Am Grateful

_____

_____

Nightly Note to Self

_____

_____

_____

MORNING

Dreams

_____

_____

_____

_____

_____

_____

_____

_____

Steps I Will Take to Reach My Weekly Goal

_____

_____

_____

_____

Luck is not chance, it's toil; fortune's expensive smile is earned.
~Emily Dickinson

NIGHT

Daily Summary

_____

_____

_____

_____

_____

_____

_____

_____

Tomorrow's To-Do List

_____

_____

_____

4 Things for Which I Am Grateful

_____

_____

Nightly Note to Self

_____

_____

_____

_____

MORNING

Dreams

_____

_____

_____

_____

_____

_____

_____

_____

Steps I Will Take to Reach My Weekly Goal

_____

_____

_____

_____

We are such stuff s dreams are made on
  ~William Shakespeare

NIGHT

Daily Summary

_____

_____

_____

_____

_____

_____

_____

_____

Tomorrow's To-Do List

_____

_____

_____

_____

4 Things for Which I Am Grateful

_____

_____

Nightly Note to Self

_____

_____

_____

_____

MORNING

Dreams

_____

_____

_____

_____

_____

_____

_____

_____

Steps I Will Take to Reach My Weekly Goal

_____

_____

_____

_____

Look at situations from all angles, and you will become more open.
~Dalai Lama

NIGHT

Daily Summary

_____

_____

_____

_____

_____

_____

_____

_____

Tomorrow's To-Do List

_____

_____

_____

4 Things for Which I Am Grateful

_____

_____

Nightly Note to Self

_____

_____

_____

_____

MORNING

Dreams

_____

_____

_____

_____

_____

_____

_____

_____

Steps I Will Take to Reach My Weekly Goal

_____

_____

_____

_____

_____

I prefer to be true to myself, even at the hazard of incurring the ridicule of others, rather than to be false, and to incur my own abhorrence.

~Frederick Douglass

NIGHT

Daily Summary

_____

_____

_____

_____

_____

_____

_____

_____

_____

Tomorrow's To-Do List

_____

_____

_____   _____

4 Things for Which I Am Grateful

_____   _____

Nightly Note to Self

_____

_____

_____

_____

MORNING

Dreams

_____

_____

_____

_____

_____

_____

_____

_____

_____

Steps I Will Take to Reach My Weekly Goal

_____

_____

_____

_____

_____

When you can do the common things of life in an uncommon way, you will command the attention of the world.
~George Washington Carver

NIGHT

Daily Summary

_____

_____

_____

_____

_____

_____

_____

_____

Tomorrow's To-Do List

_____

_____

_____

_____

4 Things for Which I Am Grateful

_____

_____

Nightly Note to Self

_____

_____

_____

_____

MONTHLY PLANNER

Week 1 Goals

Week 2 Goals

Week 3 Goals

Week 4 Goals

WEEKLY PLANNER

Weekly Goals

My Accomplishments

Special Dates/Events

MORNING

Dreams

_____
_____
_____
_____
_____
_____
_____
_____
_____

Steps I Will Take to Reach My Weekly Goal

_____
_____
_____
_____
_____

Just don't give up trying to do what you really want to do. Where there is love and inspiration, I don't think you can go wrong.
~Ella Fitzgerald

NIGHT

Daily Summary

_____

_____

_____

_____

_____

_____

_____

_____

_____

Tomorrow's To-Do List

_____

_____

_____

_____

4 Things for Which I Am Grateful

_____

_____

Nightly Note to Self

_____

_____

_____

_____

205

MORNING

Dreams

_____

_____

_____

_____

_____

_____

_____

Steps I Will Take to Reach My Weekly Goal

_____

_____

_____

_____

First thing every morning before you arise say out loud, 'I believe,' three times.

~Ovid

NIGHT

Daily Summary

_____

_____

_____

_____

_____

_____

_____

_____

Tomorrow's To-Do List

_____

_____

_____

4 Things for Which I Am Grateful

_____

_____

Nightly Note to Self

_____

_____

_____

_____

MORNING

Dreams

_____

_____

_____

_____

_____

_____

_____

_____

Steps I Will Take to Reach My Weekly Goal

_____

_____

_____

_____

Belief creates the actual fact.
   ~William James

NIGHT

Daily Summary

_____

_____

_____

_____

_____

_____

_____

_____

Tomorrow's To-Do List

_____

_____

_____

_____

4 Things for Which I Am Grateful

_____

_____

Nightly Note to Self

_____

_____

_____

_____

MORNING

Dreams

_____

_____

_____

_____

_____

_____

_____

_____

_____

Steps I Will Take to Reach My Weekly Goal

_____

_____

_____

_____

To avoid criticism, do nothing, say nothing, and be nothing.
~Elbert Hubbard

NIGHT

Daily Summary

_____

_____

_____

_____

_____

_____

_____

Tomorrow's To-Do List

_____

_____

_____

_____

4 Things for Which I Am Grateful

_____

_____

Nightly Note to Self

_____

_____

_____

_____

MORNING

Dreams

_____

_____

_____

_____

_____

_____

_____

_____

Steps I Will Take to Reach My Weekly Goal

_____

_____

_____

_____

Happiness is neither virtue nor pleasure nor this thing nor that
but simply growth, We are happy when we are growing.
   ~William Butler Yeats

NIGHT

Daily Summary

_____
_____
_____
_____
_____
_____
_____
_____
_____

Tomorrow's To-Do List

_____   _____
_____   _____
_____   _____
_____

4 Things for Which I Am Grateful

_____   _____
_____   _____

Nightly Note to Self

_____
_____
_____
_____

MORNING

Dreams

_____

_____

_____

_____

_____

_____

_____

_____

Steps I Will Take to Reach My Weekly Goal

_____

_____

_____

_____

_____

Happiness is not something ready-made. It comes from your own actions.

~Dalai Lama

NIGHT

Daily Summary

_____

_____

_____

_____

_____

_____

_____

_____

Tomorrow's To-Do List

_____

_____

_____

4 Things for Which I Am Grateful

_____

_____

Nightly Note to Self

_____

_____

_____

_____

MORNING

Dreams

_____

_____

_____

_____

_____

_____

_____

_____

Steps I Will Take to Reach My Weekly Goal

_____

_____

_____

_____

_____

Boldness be my friend.
~William Shakespeare

NIGHT

Daily Summary

_____

_____

_____

_____

_____

_____

_____

_____

Tomorrow's To-Do List

_____

_____

_____

_____

4 Things for Which I Am Grateful

_____

_____

Nightly Note to Self

_____

_____

_____

_____

WEEKLY PLANNER

Weekly Goals

My Accomplishments

Special Dates/Events

NOTES

MORNING

Dreams

_____

_____

_____

_____

_____

_____

_____

Steps I Will Take to Reach My Weekly Goal

_____

_____

_____

_____

_____

Light tomorrow with today!
~Elizabeth Barrett Browning

NIGHT

Daily Summary

_____

_____

_____

_____

_____

_____

_____

_____

Tomorrow's To-Do List

_____

_____

_____

_____

4 Things for Which I Am Grateful

_____

_____

Nightly Note to Self

_____

_____

_____

_____

MORNING

Dreams

_____

_____

_____

_____

_____

_____

_____

_____

Steps I Will Take to Reach My Weekly Goal

_____

_____

_____

_____

_____

Life is a journey. When we stop, things don't go right.
~Pope Francis

NIGHT

Daily Summary

_____

_____

_____

_____

_____

_____

_____

Tomorrow's To-Do List

_____

_____

_____

4 Things for Which I Am Grateful

_____

_____

Nightly Note to Self

_____

_____

_____

_____

MORNING

Dreams

_____

_____

_____

_____

_____

_____

_____

_____

Steps I Will Take to Reach My Weekly Goal

_____

_____

_____

_____

_____

The secret of getting ahead is getting started.
~ Mark Twain

NIGHT

Daily Summary

_____

_____

_____

_____

_____

_____

_____

_____

Tomorrow's To-Do List

_____

_____

_____

4 Things for Which I Am Grateful

_____

_____

Nightly Note to Self

_____

_____

_____

_____

MORNING

Dreams

_____

_____

_____

_____

_____

_____

_____

Steps I Will Take to Reach My Weekly Goal

_____

_____

_____

_____

This above all; to thine own self be true.
~William Shakespeare

NIGHT

Daily Summary

_____

_____

_____

_____

_____

_____

_____

_____

Tomorrow's To-Do List

_____

_____

_____ _____

_____

4 Things for Which I Am Grateful

_____ _____

_____

Nightly Note to Self

_____

_____

_____

_____

MORNING

Dreams

_____

_____

_____

_____

_____

_____

_____

_____

Steps I Will Take to Reach My Weekly Goal

_____

_____

_____

_____

In order to carry a positive action we must develop here a positive vision.

~Dalai Lama

NIGHT

Daily Summary

_____

_____

_____

_____

_____

_____

_____

_____

Tomorrow's To-Do List

_____

_____

_____

_____

4 Things for Which I Am Grateful

_____

_____

Nightly Note to Self

_____

_____

_____

_____

MORNING

Dreams

_____

_____

_____

_____

_____

_____

_____

_____

Steps I Will Take to Reach My Weekly Goal

_____

_____

_____

_____

We are shaped by our thoughts; we become what we think. When the mind is pure, joy follows like a shadow that never leaves.
~Buddha

NIGHT

Daily Summary

_____

_____

_____

_____

_____

_____

_____

_____

Tomorrow's To-Do List

_____

_____

_____   _____

4 Things for Which I Am Grateful

_____   _____

_____

Nightly Note to Self

_____

_____

_____

_____

MORNING

Dreams

_____

_____

_____

_____

_____

_____

_____

_____

Steps I Will Take to Reach My Weekly Goal

_____

_____

_____

_____

Do not dwell in the past, do not dream of the future, concentrate
the mind on the present moment.

~ Buddha

NIGHT

Daily Summary

_____

_____

_____

_____

_____

_____

_____

_____

Tomorrow's To-Do List

_____

_____

_____

_____

4 Things for Which I Am Grateful

_____

_____

Nightly Note to Self

_____

_____

_____

_____

ASSESS YOUR PROGRESS

Are there any changes you need to make in your approach? Have some of your priorities shifted?

Health/Exercise

Career

Creativity

Finances

Relationships

Spiritual life

Hobbies/Leisure

———————————

Weekly Goals

My Accomplishments

Special Dates/Events

Printed in the United States
By Bookmasters